The Black and White Days

The Black and White Days

poems by
Vernon Scannell

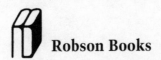

Robson Books

First published in Great Britain in 1996 by Robson
Books Ltd, Bolsover House, 5–6 Clipstone Street,
London W1P 8LE

British Library Cataloguing in Publication Data
A catalogue record for this title is available from
the British Library

ISBN 1 86105 020 8

Set in Trump Mediaeval by Columns Design Ltd.,
Reading
Printed and bound by T. J. Press (Padstow) Ltd.,
Padstow, Cornwall

Acknowledgements

Acknowledgements are due to the editors of the following journals in which many of the poems collected in this volume first appeared:

Ambit, the *London Magazine*, *Medicine and War*, the *Observer*, *Outposts*, *PN Review*, *Poetry Review*, *Seam*, the *Spectator*, *Stand*, the *Sunday Times*, *The Times* and *The Times Literary Supplement*.

'Dominoes' and 'Junk' are reprinted from *Catch the Light* (OUP) and 'Makers and Creatures' is from *The Apple Raid* (Chatto & Windus).

Contents

The First Piano on the Moon

has not been launched as yet, but it could be.
It's not past human ingenuity
to anchor it on some bleak lunar sea.
The vision and intelligence of man
has not shown evidence more powerful than
the presence of the thing itself, which can
be marvelled at for what it does yet seen
not only as a wonderful machine
but as aesthetic object. It could stand
in frozen silence and be no less grand.

Of course, like every dazzling artefact,
it did not suddenly appear intact
but it evolved; the simple dulcimer
was probably its earliest ancestor.
To me, more magical than *Gemini 8*
or Russian *Soyuz 10*, its intricate
fine mechanism: damper, check and spring,
the wires and pivot-point, everything
concealed behind dark gleam of wood in which
the keys lie white as milk and black as pitch.

So dream of it, lid lifted to beguile
a future astronaut with its fixed smile.
Quite possible, by then, he would not know
what purpose this device once served, although
he'd never doubt that it was made by man,
but hardly guess that parts of it began
as bits of mammoth and its habitat,
nor, in that sterile silence, realise that,
held in this graceful engine's wooden chest,
chained, sonic constellations, glittering, rest.

Elgar Louts

Their favourite season is autumn
When the Malverns seem to shift
Slightly sideways in the morning mist
And the chill of the wind
Is tempered by a breath
Of leafmeal's sweet decay.

This is when they come
Cavorting down the slopes
Waving their Union Jacks, their eyes
Gleaming, moist, as if each sees
Visions of white cenotaphs
And sacrificial deeds.

In the village inn they raise
Their tankards and drink deep
To yellowing memories
Of bugle-calls and battlefields
And swear that they can hear
The far off thunder of the guns.

And later, after dark, before
The final call of time
When everyone's at least half-pissed
They weep like candles for the lost
And golden girl, that drift of hair
In cello-light, the secret smile.

Bare arms and shoulders, fluent, white;
Thoughtful fingers coaxing sighs
And soft melodious moans from strings;
All the gleam and glimmer gone
With Olaf and Caractacus
And the Worcester Asylum Band.

Fin de Siècle

All handsome or, at least, they have their charm,
A college elegance, insouciant grace;
They lounge on pampered turf and every face
Is smiling, dreamily perhaps, quite calm,
Oblivious of any lurking harm.
In light like lemonade each takes his place,
And knows he owns far more than that small space,
Unruffled by the slightest doubt or qualm.

Before the darkness falls they must decide
Exactly where their marvellous talents lie –
Poet, statesman, wit or spiritual guide –
Though none can prophesy or try to cheat
The various ways that they will have to die
Of bravery, boredom or the spirochaete.

Magnum Opus

In Memoriam Jacob Kramer 1892–1962

One night in The Victoria in Leeds
Jacob said to me, 'Before I die
I'm going to paint a picture that will stun
them all. They think I've lost
whatever talent I once had,
that drink and craziness have neutered me.
I'll prove them wrong.
It's going to be a northern landscape,
forests, mountains, peaks, a pitiless sky –
but non-specific, if you follow me –
a landscape of the heart.
It's haunted me for years.
I'll show you ... look ...'

And on the surface of the bar
he slopped a little of his beer
and with one spatulate forefinger drew
the soaring outline of the mountain-range.

'And here,' he muttered, wheezing, 'down below
in darker tones are hooded figures,
or they could be trees, or both ... you see?'

I stared and for a spell-bound moment glimpsed
the apocalyptic vision Jacob saw.
And then the barman's damp and grimy cloth
came swishing down and wiped the lot away.
'Drink up now gents, it's way past time,' he said.
'I reckon all of us should be in bed.'

5

The Black and White Days

Not only dreams were shot in black and white
But all the wide-eyed world of day and night;
    The music, too,
As black and white as piano keyboard or
Bleached tuxes and black ties the band all wore,
    Whose each jet shoe
That tapped the ragtime out would always show
A small pale highlight gleaming on the toe,
    And you could tell
The Leader by the large carnation which,
Like a curled-up spider, black as pitch,
    Slept on his white lapel.

The hat-check girls in fishnet tights applied
Dark lipstick to their mouths that looked like dried
    Blood or paint
Against white skin and sugar-icing teeth;
The blonde-haired singer wore a tight black sheath
    From whose constraint
The smooth-as-candle flesh flowed out and swelled
In bosom, tapering arms, and hands that held
    Sad emptiness
As blues' slow lamentations drifted round
Her silver-haloed head, deep midnight sound
    Of smoky, sweet distress.

The days of black and white, of sniffed cocaine,
Black guns and hard-boiled shirt fronts shocked with stain
    Like spreading ink,
Black blood, small maps of doomed desires, and fears,
Mad loyalties, betrayals, kisses, tears,
    The molls in mink,
Mascara smeared; the sidewalks in the rain
Varnished by lamps that laid a silver chain,
    Reflected light,
Across black paving where the gangsters died.
And checkered concrete blocks soared up to hide
    Night skies from sight.

But surely those were shadows on a screen?
This multicoloured world has never been
    Like that at all.
Did not gold lights gush in, rich curtains close?
Well, yes, the anthem played and we all rose,
    Yet I recall,
As we filed slowly out on whispering feet
And reached the almost silent, city street,
    Where all the bars
And shops were dark and shut, we started back
Beneath a natural sky, nun's-habit black,
    Sprinkled with salt of stars.

Farewell Performance

Glos: 0, let me kiss that hand!
Lear: Let me wipe it first; it smells of mortality.

King Lear

Shuffle of shoes, scrape and creak, voices
Murmur, a woman laughs, then lights are doused
And darkness floods the hall and drowns all noise;
The platform and the piano, though, are hosed
With dazzling lather and the keyboard smiles.

It smiles and waits. The old man makes his entrance,
Moving slowly on uncertain feet,
A mobile hawthorn, gnarled and blackened, bent,
So slow we think he'll never reach his seat;
To him the walk must seem to cover miles.

And from the bright-lit platform a faint odour
Of sweet decay drifts in the staring air
As he attains the stool. He is so old
Applause might be for his arriving there.
His head is bowed so we can't see his eyes,

And if the ancient skull were turned towards us
Dark sockets might direct their empty gaze
From where he settles at the keyboard. Pause
Of taut anxiety before he plays,
Then apprehension melts, and pity dies.

We hear the Liszt Sonata in B minor
Flow and ripple through compliant space
To work sly sorcery along the spine
And pierce the heart with that familiar grace
Of truth and love that brook no compromise.

His hands dance on the keys; the nimble fingers
Are young as they cavort, caress, compel
Involuntary surrender while they sing
Of bliss and melancholy, heaven and hell;
It is not their mortality we smell.

Dirigible

Summer of 1930 in Eccles:
An eight-year-old boy was bowling his hoop
On the cobbles, a rusty and spokeless rim
Of a bicycle wheel; it bounced and rattled
Down Bardsley Street between the dark rows
Of crouching houses. A buttercup sun
In a clean blue sky. The boy was on holiday.

He was alone in the street, but not for long:
Solitude burst in a gaping of doors,
Loud callings and laughter; a flutter of dusters,
Aprons and towels, a festival feeling,
Everyone pointing and peering skywards,
Hands shading eyes like peaks of caps.
The boy let his hoop fall with a clatter.

And he, like the others, stared upwards, his mouth
As wide as his eyes as he saw the thing come
High over the roofs, bumbling, benign,
An enormous prize marrow, lacquered with silver,
The sunlight slithering over its skin,
Those weightless tons floating, preposterous and beautiful:
'It's the R One Hundred and One!' cried a woman.

Now he could hear its five engines drumming
As it floated closer, at last loomed directly
Over their heads. It did not seem possible
That men had devised it, were even now watching
From seats in the gondola under its belly:

To the boy it was magical, a wingless marvel,
A skyborne leviathan floating on nothing.

He stayed in the street long after the wonder
Had passed out of sight and the other spectators
Were back in the unenchanted places,
The sunless sculleries of mangle and copper
And chores of any ordinary morning,
He stayed and he stared as if the blue heavens
Might still be embossed with a trace of its presence.

Weeks later, when summer had ripened and fallen
And evenings came early with sad smoky breath,
The news of disaster fluttered the leaves
In gutter and parlour; the boy saw the smudged
And desolate picture, the huge fallen creature,
Black skeleton of girders scattered and broken,
The silvery skin consumed by the flames.

It had crashed on a hillside in France. It would never
Rise from its ashes and ride high again
And shine in the skies over Eccles, although
A ghost of its body hung shimmering and pale
In the sky in the skull of the Bardsley Street boy,
Would stay there, impervious to time and to gravity,
Melding to myth that no flames could destroy.

Family Secret

An old man now,
He roots among the rubble in the dark
Where dusty images of childhood lurk
Observing how
They are uncovered by some sensuous whim,
A trick of evening light surprising him
Before soft slam of night,
Tobacco-wraith and candle-smoke,
The wistful aspiration of violin.

A sepia close-up:
His father's face with joke moustache, eyes meek
Yet mischievous beneath the cheeky peak
Of service-cap;
Killed in France before his child was born.
No picture of the mother. She had gone
Peculiar, they said,
And disappeared. She must be dead
And buried long ago, the grave not known.

That's how he came
To live with Grannie, Grandpa and, of course,
The two huge uncles in the gaslit house
In Cuthbert Lane.
So many shapes and shades, such fears and joys,
Sly ambiguities; the distant noise
Of no-man's-land was heard
Behind domestic chimes of chores,
Low grumble of big guns and bugle-calls.

One afternoon
Grannie, with the kettle, making tea,
Splashed some boiling water on his knee.
The scalding wound
Howled loud and, later, when the swollen hurt
Was dressed and eased, though sobs still sputtered out,
One of the uncles said,
'Be a brave soldier, lad!' The boy
Gulped back his tears: 'I will. Just like my Dad!'

The kitchen blinked.
It held its breath; the silence clamped down hard.
He felt as if he'd said a wicked word,
But could not think
What it could be. He knew that it was he
Who'd frozen every sound. Then suddenly
His Grannie laughed and tried
To sweep unease away, although
The boy still felt perturbed and mystified.

What they all knew
He feels they should have told him long ago
Before deluded pride and love had swollen so.
This much is true:
His Dad had been no hero but a child,
A frightened boy who'd sprawled face-down in mud
With no salutes, no wild
Or mournful bugle-calls, no flags,
But dawn's death-rattle of the firing-squad.

Compulsory Mourning

M described his treatment of tank commanders who had lost crews and were unwilling to command another tank as 'compulsory mourning'. He arranged for them '... to be confined to a small darkened room for three days with an order to mourn and blunt statements were made about their selfishness ... they were fed on water and bread alone and were allowed one hour's daylight and one hour's electric light a day.'

From a report on 'The Northfield Experiment', a survey of psychiatric treatment given to soldiers in Northfield Military Hospital, Birmingham 1940–47

I lie in darkness on this bed of stone.
The shrewd cold bites like acid to the bone
And I am sick with gelded rage and hate,
And something I can't quite define – a weight
Of guilt, a bitter taste, and then the flood
Of concentrated loathing, dark as blood,
Surges through me and it leaves behind,
Among the sludge and lumber in the mind,
An image, vast and vivid, of his face,
Plump, well-shaven, showing not a trace
Of doubt or sympathy, this man who claims
That he's not hoodwinked by my little games,
And sees with X-ray eyes through walls of bone
Inside the haunted skull, and he alone
Can teach me how to mourn as I should do
The charred and blackened things that were my crew.
I think of his soft hands, like pastry dough,

And how they'd spit and sizzle in the glow
Inside the turret of a brewed-up tank.

The dead can't smell themselves – at least I pray
To Christ they can't! How terrible if they
Not only have to bear, but be their smell
For ever more in some peculiar hell!
That smell is in my nostrils, seems to spread
Inside my mouth and throat, it's in my head.
And with it come the voices of the war,
The glint of pain and terror through the roar
Of our Crusader's engine and the shrill
Static, Morse and jamming noise that spill
From radio to season this rich din;
And, from outside, the almost childish, thin
Rattle of machine guns and blunt thud
Of eighty-eights. And then the tune of blood,
A soft insistent note, a kind of sigh
That lingers when the other voices die
And is ubiquitous. It joins the scent
Of cooking human flesh, is redolent
Of war and all that means, and ever meant.

In my protracted night the hours are melled
Into a timeless slur and I am held
By links of frozen minutes to a stake
Of impotence and anger. Though awake
I can't escape the images and sounds
That rise from nightmare's heaving burial grounds.
But I'll survive. And, furthermore, *his* scorn
And punitive attempts to make me mourn
The cinders of my crew will never crack
This resolution never to go back
And do it all again. In just three days
I'll rise from here and walk into the blaze
Of morning sunshine like the third day lad,
The Son of Man, and I shall swear I've had
A change of heart, that now my single aim

Is vengeance on the swine who are to blame
For my dead comrades' fate. Then he will claim
A medical and military success,
And he'll be wrong again. My readiness
To soldier on will be a trickster's act,
But he'll be fooled and swallow it as fact,
Hooked by his vanity. As for my crew,
I'm sure they'd both endorse my point of view.
I see them now: Chalky, my driver, hard
Middleweight from Bethnal Green, with scarred
Eyebrows, flattened nose, and such a flow
Of hoarse profanity you'd never know
That he was just nineteen and that below
The carapace of toughness you would find
A gentleness surprising as the mind,
That in the worst of crises, understood
The situation as I rarely could;
He'd grunt his practical advice although
He never let a glimpse of smugness show,
Nor hinted that he thought that he should be
Commander of the tank instead of me.
The gunner, Jim, complete antithesis
Of Chalky but, maybe because of this,
His steadfast mucker, rarely said a word
And, when he did, the tone of voice you heard
Was mild as butter, mellow from the green
Devon hills and fields, the words as clean
As Sunday linen though, when we attacked,
Or were ourselves attacked, he would react
With steely competence and seem to be
A cool extension of the gun that he
With steady concentration aimed and fired.

And now, the man, who thinks he holds a key
To wind his soldiers up and then decree
That they be used again in lethal games,
Must be dismissed as, in the dark, your names,
Chalky and Jim, turn slowly in my mind,

Those unburnt syllables. I hope I'll find
A way to make them breathe. Meanwhile I try
To coax oblivion to where I lie
And roll between my forefinger and thumb
A piece of bread, no bigger than a crumb,
Until it is an amuletic ball
With magic properties that might forestall
Invasion of those images which maul
The unprotected consciousness when sleep
Takes full command and I no longer keep
My regimental mask secure, in place,
And wake at dawn to find my human face
Smeared and wet with tears. *He* must not see
That shameful nakedness exposed, for he
Would claim success for his experiment.
Being as stupid as malevolent
He would not know, nor will he ever know
Those saline exclamation-marks don't show
My mourning, as he understands the word –
No impulse to avenge will have occurred –
Just speechless sorrow as the grit of guilt
That can't, however many tears are spilt,
Be washed away. I shall not fight again.
There are no accusations from the slain,
Nor will there ever be; yet, when that's said,
The spirits or the shadows of the dead
Must be petitioned and appeased. I pray
Into the unresponsive dark that they,
My better, braver, comrades will forgive
Not just this unheroic urge to live
(Small doubt of that) but chiefly this regret
That I must bear the burden and the boon
Of living on beyond their brief forenoon.
I think that they would wish me to rejoice
Without regret and would approve my choice
Of opting for old age in civvy street.
I hope that's so.
                    I don't suppose we'll meet
In some celestial boozer later on,

But one thing is for sure: when I have gone
From this infernal place I may well find
Myself not drinking at, but stuck behind,
Bars of the uncongenial, penal kind.
But I'll get out and then I'll drink to you –
Chalky and Jim – and this I hope is true:
As long as I am able to survive,
While I still breathe, I'll keep you two alive.

El Alamein: 50th Anniversary, October 1992

Fifty years! He's old and out of sorts
But still he smiles to see them on the screen,
The lads they were, tin hats, enormous shorts
As big as bivouacs. Full magazine,
One up the spout, going in at the high-port
Through smoke, a newsreel shot in black and white;
A fake for civvies, so he'd always thought;
It wasn't cameras shooting that first night.

And then live interviews – well, just about –
Old men, false teeth and medals, pretty toys
Dangling from their ribbons. Gaunt or stout
They wheeze or croak. Fade out. He hears the noise
Of bugle's rhetoric; then words: *Lest we forget.*
He snorts; then wonders why his face is wet.

A Cemetery Revisited

He has been here before, to this old church
And freshly barbered garden of the dead.
It's almost fifty years since he dug in
And crouched among the consecrated mounds
Marked by stones, not these white lozenges
Paraded here in strict geometries
But ancient, poxed and mossy sepulchres.
At night the mortars and machine-gun fire
Could not quite still the rattling of the cold
White branches of the old ones buried there.

He was one of a small company, though each
Man knew he was alone and wore the same
Coarse battledress of prickly fear and each
Released from queasy heart and lips the same
And nursery prayer which like a tiny rocket
Tried to climb the lacerated sky
Towards a deity who might not yet
Be stunned and deafened by the din below
Of eighty-eights and Nebelwerfers' howls,
Or worse, not deaf,but grown indifferent.

And so he has returned, an old man now.
In autumn's elegiac sunlight he patrols
The files of white stone tablets reading names
And regiments; a few bear pious verses;
Some are nameless, each of these inscribed
Known only unto God. Well, yes, perhaps
Those jigsaw bits of bone and ragged flesh

Have all been reassembled in God's head,
A kind of *carnis resurrectionem*.
He turns away, then sees the woman there.

She stands quite still among the rows of graves.
Unnoticed he draws closer, then he sees,
Surprised, her face though turned away from him
Is young, a girl's soft cheek. His heart is tripped
By tender shock to see the wash of tears.
She is too young for mourning yet she weeps,
Perhaps for all the pain and waste of war.
He turns and walks away, does not look back
But knows she'll stay there, patient and alone,
Her tears like scattered seeds on obdurate stone.

On Lovers' Walk: 1939

A warm and moon-splashed night on Lovers' Walk,
One war ended, the other not begun;
No noise at closing-time from Belial's boys
Clattering on the cobbles of the Square
South of the border down Mexico way,
Or anywhere; no spies to know that he
Is trembling as she murmurs, moans and moves
Compliant to his touch, mouth opening
Beneath his own; he tastes faint apple-scent
That mingles with a something from the sea
And with a sweetness, too, that hints a rhyme
For lilac trembling in the webby air;
And then his blind and breathless hand is led
To where it meets the source of that small flood,
A melted moon-beam long since drowned and dredged
Emulsive from a deep Sargasso bed,
And he and she are gathered up and flung
Spinning where the constellations wheel.
Dumb thunders shake the skies until the spell
Is spent and they descend to earth and feel
The stillness settle round them like a shawl.
Next morning as he walks to work he sees
The sky squeegeed, unblemished, limpid blue,
A palimpsest of possibility.
On Lovers' Walk the lilac trembles still
And there among the dewy clusters hangs
In naked light a pale and slippery thing,

A slug-like creature at first glance, then seen
For what it is: a grey, translucent bag,
Not large, poetic or American,
Though probably containing multitudes.

Refugees

In dusk of helmet-brims the eyes look stern,
Unwavering; no matter what they see
Or where they gaze – Bluff Cove, Thermopoylae,
Kuwait, the Somme – the pillaged cities burn,
And when the owners of those eyes return
And put away their weapons there will be
An alien music in a harsher key,
New words and syntax difficult to learn.

Wars never end. Across the livid plain
The dark processions trail, the refugees,
Anonymous beneath indifferent skies,
Somnambulistic, patient shapes of pain,
Long commentary on war, an ancient frieze
Of figures we refuse to recognise.

The Searchers

We see them on the television-screen,
Each shrunk by distance to a manikin,
Lined up across the moor. They seem to lean
Against the raking wind as they begin
Their slow advance; at every pace they pause
And plunge into the earth before their toes
Their sharpened sticks; then each of them withdraws
His pointed probe and lifts it to his nose.
We know that they are sniffing for a trace
Of carrion from the scabbard of the ground,
And somewhere in that God-forsaken place
The murdered children lie and must be found.

Not on the screen but being watched by it
The man and woman move about the room,
Lift ornaments and put them down, then sit,
Though only briefly, in the curtained gloom,
Until they rise again and climb the stairs
And prowl around the house. They do not speak
And neither sees the pain the other bears,
Nor understands that what they both now seek,
In dazed, somnambulistic wandering
From room to room, will never be revealed:
Forgiveness, that intolerable thing,
Which all their guilt and suffering will not yield.

Old Man in Love

Cocktail of music and wonder dizzies the heart;
Rustle of waters behind the bridal foam,
Voicing various choices never known
Beyond the boundaries of dream or art
Unreels a sonic filament of gold
On which the glittering syllables are hung:
'Oh my dear,' he breathes, 'this love is young,
Although the vessel that it brims is old!'

And, septuagenarian, he capers, sings,
And all that he can carol, call or cry
Is love, the rapturous young love that brings
Him here, to this vertiginously high
Peak of joy where, arms flung wide like wings,
Drunk with his luck, he swears that he could fly.

A Love Song

I've always been in love with you I swear.
'Impossible,' they say, yet it is true:
I speak with certainty, for I was there.

When I reeled groggy as the punchbowl air
Was spiced with melody I longed for you;
I've always been in love with you I swear.

My infant whispers to the beat-up bear
Were meant for you, the tears and kisses too;
I speak with certainty, for I was there.

Let experts, calendars and maps declare
I'm nuts or have at least one wobbly screw;
I've always been in love with you I swear.

New kinds of beauty and the wish to share
These riches were rehearsals, as I knew;
I speak with certainty, for I was there.

Those shadow-loves were work-outs to prepare
For this, the main event, that they led to:
I've always been in love with you I swear;
I speak with certainty, for I was there.

Calculations

All those delicious dancers, the women,
Dreamed temptresses, the shadows on screens;
Sepia-toned goddesses with bald pudenda,
Each breast, like a porcelain-coated half lemon,
Dappled by foliage in hot magazines,
Even now their memory is able to send a
Shadowy shiver from my early teens.

Also, from novels and poems, I listed
More feminine qualities I could applaud,
And hoped to discover them parcelled in real
Huggable flesh. And so I insisted
No one, except an amalgam of Maud,
Beatrice and Keats' Isabella could steal
My heart from its moorings and tempt it abroad.

When you ask me today, if I find, when I tot
Up the various assets embodied in you,
Every perfection, heroic and lyrical,
How nice to say yes; but it wouldn't be true;
You'd fail as my nonpareil by a long shot,
If the heart's calculations were mathematical
Which, luckily, darling, we both know they're not.

Daily Mail

Morning. Almost nine o'clock. I hear
The metal snap of letter-box, the flop
And skitter on the mat behind the door
    And feel at once the small
Match-like flickering of hope and fear,
Minute, yet still with power enough to stop
The heartbeat for a wink of time before
    I go into the hall.

The usual stuff: I see that I've again
Been chosen to enjoy a holiday
In Tenerife, the latest Ford Gazelle,
    Or fifteen grand in cash;
I'm asked to take my pick, but I refrain.
Nor am I tempted by a fortnight's stay
In Cairo's most luxurious hotel.
    I riffle through the trash:

Invest in Humbro with no risk at all,
Reminders, bills, appeals for *Bosnia Aid*,
CD Classic Club, *The Best of Swing*,
    A postcard from Peru
Signed warmly by a name I can't recall.
A quick re-check as hope begins to fade,
Will die, unless the second post should bring
    That word of love from you.

Bathtimes

i

A strange bath in a small hotel in Durham,
Old fashioned, long, like a porcelain coffin,
He lolls in it and lingers,
Watches, with detachment, pubic hair,
Sparse kelp, thin scrawl on water.
He tries to recollect its dark abundance
When he was young and muscular, but fails,
Or, rather, he recalls it in the head alone
As one remembers dates or names of people
Which freeze, discarnate, in the mind.
He lets his gaze
Drift down to where his toes are visible,
Breaking the steaming surface, and observes
How long his toenails are. They seem to grow
More quickly now as they, he understands,
Will go on growing after he is dead.
The treacherous little bastards are rehearsing.
He nods and smiles a faint sour smile,
And they grin back at him quite equably,
Without the faintest smidgin of remorse.

ii

Another bathroom, familiar, his own:
Arctic white of basin, bowl and tub
Is gentled by a fragrant mist;
Silver taps and towel-rail gleam and sweat.
Small waves lap over him.

Promontories of knees protrude like knolls,
The rest of him lagooned, a coral reef.
He stays until the water cools,
Then heaves himself erect,
Reaches for towel and steps on to the mat.
As he begins to dry himself he's pierced
By tiny shock, quick as a single pulse-beat,
The knowledge of another presence there,
And from the corner of his heart he sees,
Behind the film of moisture curtaining
The full-length mirror, movement, form,
A naked woman lifting both her hands
To touch her hair, that lovely gesture like
A Roman amphora made of glowing flesh.
With one swift sweep of towel he wipes the glass
To face a bare and gaunt old man who stares
With still astonished, briefly youthful eyes.

Near the Cliff's Edge

Near the cliff's edge, high above
The restless, dark, white-stippled sea,
A man and woman walk as one;
Their languid steps rhyme perfectly.

The sun is loverlike, is fierce
And yet caressing, jealous too,
Will not permit a single white
Intruder to disturb the blue.

Gorse sweetens the warm soft breeze.
The man and woman pause to kiss
And then move on. Suddenly
He feels disquiet he can't dismiss,

A chilling breath, a faceless fear,
And in this English sun can't guess
Why, amid green abundance, he
Should glimpse a white, blind wilderness,

Great plains of snow and ice, recall
That somewhere he has read or heard
Of two doomed travellers who sensed
The presence of a nameless third.

Love Poet

Of all the poets of his generation
He best explored love's ecstasy and pain,
And overheard the wordless conversation
Of gaze with gaze, and made its meaning plain.

In glinting lyrics, delicate and witty,
He linked the syllables and made a chain
Of images of longing, rage and pity
That shimmered in each reader's heart and brain.

His tolerance and reconciliation
Of opposite emotions seemed divine;
Imagine, then, the general consternation

When he fell sick, grew pale, began to pine,
And failed to diagnose his own condition:
On love he never wrote another line.

Love Lasting

'Love never has lasted for ever,'
   The grey philospher said,
'Whatever your senses might promise
   Or the poems and novels you've read.

'Like those delectable goodies
   We sucked on when we were young,
Though it lasts a little bit longer,
   It melts quickly away on the tongue.

'And though a faint hint of the flavour
   May linger awhile, when you bite
On another rich chocolate or toffee,
   It's dismissed by this fresher delight.'

'He is wrong,' said the poet to lover,
   'Ignore all that cynical rot;
I know that loves *does* last for ever.
   It is lovers alas, who do not.'

Easter Visit

I slipped out of the laundered day and left it there,
Hanging outside the great glass doors to air,
Walked down long corridors that smelt of meals
Or ghosts of meals, past stillnesses on wheels.
I carried gifts of chocolates and fruit,
A yellow fanfare bright against dark suit,
Flowers of resurrection time. I stepped
Dainty through the ward, as one adept
In crossing mined terrain, and reached his bed,
Presented tributary gifts and said
A few rehearsed banalities, sat down
And grinned and nodded like a puppet clown.
I sniffed the scent of darkness in the white
Hygienic lie of air, felt flesh grow tight
On facial bone and scalp until taut skin
Made a *memento mori* of my grin.

I touched his hand and said I had to go.
I think I saw the faintest smile, although
I couldn't swear to that. 'Back soon,' I said,
And moved away with fake reluctant tread,
Then stepped up pace beyond the ward. Outside,
The air was merciless and sweet, denied
Its lightless opposite, and I breathed deep.
Against the sky the building, with a sweep
Of rough-spun shadow, darkened where I stood.
I crossed into the sun, walked fast, felt good.

Wedding Picture

He stands, arranged around his grin
Which, like his posture, seems to be
    Stiff, as if with fear;
Yet something in the lift of chin
And glint of eye suggests that he
    Is happy to be here.

It hints, too, that he thinks he's made
A fine discerning choice in this
    Slight figure at his side,
Whose timid smile might just persuade
Unworldly aunts the altar kiss
    Was all she'd ever tried.

Not so, of course, nor is it true
That he has chosen her from flocks
    Of eager candidates;
There was no breathless female queue
Of aspirants to darn his socks
    Thumping at his gates.

Like all of us, except perhaps
The very beautiful or rich,
    He takes what he can get
('Us' means girls as well as chaps)
And then proceeds to weave and stitch
    A kind of safety-net

Comprising, if not downright lies,
Elaborate hyperbole
    And sonorous pretence,
Which, with luck, might alchemise
To something much like poetry
    And make heart-piercing sense.

Birthday Counsel

For Martin Bax, August 1993

At sixty you are old enough to choose
Which path to tread and I believe you can –
Make a choice I mean – take or refuse
What's offered to the not so youthful man.
So out of bed, put on your birthday shoes,
But weigh the odds; don't move without a plan.

Well, that's one policy, the prudent way:
Go cautious to a preselected stage,
Then on towards the next without delay;
Keep clear of bars and you'll escape a cage.
Eat wholesome food, take exercise each day;
Work hard and save three-quarters of your pay.

It seems a doleful prospect, I concede,
But comfort and security must cost
The price of self-denial, though indeed
What you renounce might well be better lost.
Yet nothing can be firmly guaranteed.
However smart, you could be double-crossed.

Avoid the middle way, the worst of each.
You could try this: dive deep, though not in water;
Choose bodies, booze, and bite the sensual peach,
Savour its squirting juices, yield no quarter
In pleasure's wars; ignore the cant they preach.
This is the sweeter route, though shorter, shorter.

Climacterics

All human lives, except for those which come
With brutal prematureness to a stop
In battle, bedroom, cot or fetid slum
From virus, shrapnel or the gallows-drop,
Ordinary lives, like yours or mine,
Are seen to be, at least in retrospect –
Although they show few traces of design
Imposed by supernatural intellect –
Punctuated by climacterics
Of roughly similar contour, tint and taste.
Those spaced events, the various kicks and pricks,
Chances spurned or fatally embraced,
Moments of supreme, unhoped-for bliss,
Brief and brilliant as a rocket-burst,
Banal and haunting as a covert kiss,
Mined territory triumphantly traversed,
Or negatives of these – a frozen night
Of agony, spiked terror or despair,
Or waking to worse horror in the bright
And pitiless reveille's hostile glare –
We store in mental archives and refer
To those unfaded images when we
Long to know that change can still occur.
No matter what our present state may be,
Even in old age, hope titillates;
Change is possible and might amaze;
At least one more climacteric awaits,
The last perhaps, or so sad reason says.

Lies and Questions

There are some questions nobody should ask,
Though there is always someone to inquire,
'Is that your face or do you wear a mask?'

Whatever you reply they call you liar,
Perhaps with justice. Who for sure can tell?
Better to smile and silently retire.

The anchorite and convict share a cell;
At least the word denotes where they reside
And both could be defined by where they dwell.

But never ask what made each one decide
To turn his back on choice as both have done,
Or whether either, under oath, has lied.

And do not ask of me, or anyone,
If I would die to save a loved one pain
Or worse from sickness, torturer or gun.

For who with certainty can ascertain
If he or she would volunteer to die?
Yet it's been done and might be done again.

Though one loud 'No!' would be my firm reply
I wonder, as I say this, 'Do I lie?'

Night Reflection

Wide-angle shot: the train slides through the night,
Linked carriages, bright vertebrae. It snakes
Through fields and woods, spans rivers, roads and lakes,
Climbs hills or pierces them, going out of sight,
Then reappears and worms across the moors.
Now cut to passenger inside the train,
Alone in his compartment as the rain
Splinters on the window while he snores
Softly to the rocking of his head
From side to side, more or less in time
With flanges' iron tune and pounding rhyme.
Then sleep is splattered suddenly by dread
As violent jerk and shudder of the train
Propel him forward. When he fully wakes
Alarm dissolves: he hears the hiss of brakes
And then, more faint, susurrus of the rain.
The passenger shifts sideways, tries to stare
Through dark, smeared glass, sees nothing of what lies
Beyond but finds himself, with brief surprise,
Faced by someone gazing from out there,
With features very like his own, though more
Cadaverous. Those shadow-brimming eyes,
Their melancholy, seem to advertise
Obscure reproach which troubles him before
Another clanking spasm of the train
Distracts and strenuous wheels begin to turn.
He then discovers that he can discern
Some shadowy pattern of the dark terrain,
Vague, moving shapes of hedgerows, pylons, trees

Behind, or floating through, the spectral head
Like random and repeated thoughts which thread
A string of changing images that tease
At first, then weave their soporific spell.
Then sudden rush and rumble swallow all
In tunnel-gulp and slip impenetrable
Black against the glass, so he can't tell
Whether or not the other is still there
Concealed from him, face pressed against the pane,
Or whether swept away by driving rain;
Or could it be that that ambiguous stare
Will be confronted at the journey's end
When at the exit-barrier he will see
It waiting his arrival patiently
To claim him as accomplice, but not friend?

At the Hotel Metropole

A winter night, the city throbs and thrums.
Lights effervesce in air, or lard the streets
And, fuelled by habit, fear or appetite,
The faceless mites slide past in ones and twos.
The great hotel looms high above the park
And sleek and silent limousines arrive,
Glide silkily towards its aureate jaws,
Once there discharging fragrant skin and furs,
Swept glittering inside to leave behind
A wisp of scent, a trinket's tiny echo.

All warmth within, the foyer shimmers, glows;
Discreet servility in uniform
Greets with pious hands and lowered heads
Privilege and beauty, ushers them
Towards the restaurant where welcome waits
Orchestrally in silver, black and white:
The waiters glide glissando, bow above
Pale naked shoulders. Dishes are conveyed
And covers raised with virtuosic flourish.
Rumours of cold hunger stay outside.

Below, in basement gloom, among the pipes
And coiling wires, the building's viscera,
An alien contraption quietly ticks,
Placed there by serious men who never smile.
In time it will explode and leave behind
A brief and smoky shock of hush before
The shouts and screams, the wheeling ululations,

As medics and police press through the crowds
Who stare with curious hope but only see
Revenge's shattered logic at their feet.

Wearing Out the Dog

We discover, growing older,
April mornings are much colder,
Chilled by what once seemed mild breezes;
Also we confront new teasers
We've not had to puzzle over,
Not till now. Take my dog Rover:
He was euphemistically
'Put to sleep' in January,
Very old and sick poor chappie.
Since he went I've felt unhappy,
Missing those long walks together
We enjoyed in every weather.
Maybe I could do no better
Than to buy another setter.
Yet, despite the joy he'd give me,
He'd most probably outlive me.
That's a sobering reflection.
Here's one more for your inspection:
On my lonely walk this morning
I received a cold wet warning
From my ancient wellies telling
Me they'd sprung a leak and spelling
Out the need for their replacement,
Even in the bargain-basement
Costing plenty. See my trouble?
I'm entangled in a double
Quandary: should I decide to
Buy new boots, and if I tried to

Find a dog like my old prancer,
First I'd have to face this answer:
Which of these would wear out faster?
Boots or owner? Dog or master?

Hetta's Tail

is quite long and slender, tapering to a point,
a sleek-haired whip – appropriately, since she,
its owner, is of the whippet family.
The thing can be disposed in various ways,
curled beneath her haunches, snug between
rear legs whose shape, although she sleeps,
rehearse their tensile power in flight.
When she stretches, waking,
out it comes and, as she rises from her bed,
we see it curving from her rear,
an isolate parenthesis.
In motion it is able to command
a simple semiology,
expressing doubt or disappointment
in drooping stasis; or uncertain hope
with tentative vibrations at the tip.
More often, though, it thrashes table-legs
with rhythmic whiplash clouts
in thrilled anticipation or salute.
It is distinctive, unrelated to
the feathery wafters or blunt twitching stumps
of other breeds.
I watch her now, and she looks back at me.
A small thump on the floor. It seems to say,
'Keep things simple. No matter how you view it,
this is my tail, and I am sticking to it.'

Fictions

Fairplay's Fag

Michael Fairplay is in his study;
he toasts sausages after footer.
Outside, in wintry twilight,
Mr Clough, crow-black and mortar-boarded,
flaps across the quad in cold pursuit
of miscreants like Arnold Hughes,
the cad, who smokes expensive gaspers,
cuts morning chapel,
bribes or bullies swots to do his Latin prose.
Fairplay's fag brings jam tarts from the tuckshop
and is rewarded with a smile.
He would sooner have had a jam tart
or a sausage,
though which he would have chosen
remains pure speculation.
Later, prep and supper over,
he lies awake among striped snoozers in the dorm
and thinks of home, which is as far away
and beautiful as all of this will seem
in years to come
when he will hear again, in memory,
the owl that calls now from the ivied tower,
echoing in the dark:
Yarooh! it cries. *Yarooh! Yarooh!*

Private Dick

I quit the bar on East Thirty Second.
It is raining now and starting to get dark.
You can smell it on the sidewalk
after the heat of the past few days;
it hisses under tyres; black umbrellas
gleam slick like seals.
Two, maybe three, blocks away
a police-siren starts to howl.
Someone somewhere is getting hurt
or getting dead.
A wet evening in the city;
I carry gun and licence
and pull my dripping hat brim over eyes.
Whatever or whoever waits for me,
lurking in some alley with the trash-cans and the rats,
or smiling on a high stool in another bar,
I'm good and ready. My gun is loaded,
but I'm not. I take it easy on the sauce.
That's the way it goes
and how it always will, I guess,
leastways while I'm on a case
and that is mostly all the time.
Dumb cops foul up and I am needed then
to put things straight before the next
Missing Person, Fraud or Homicide.
I'd lay an even grand right now
my phone is ringing in the dark.

iii

Steelbrand in Mufti

Otto von Schnitzel, the master criminal,
sips Dom Perignon '79 and adjusts his monocle.
'You may leave me now,' he says to his henchman,
a hunchback possessed of preternatural strength
despite his hideous deformity,
'but do not relax for a moment your vigilance.
The Englishman could still prove troublesome.'
The Englishman is, of course, none other
than Richard Steelbrand, DSO and bar,
in mufti now the show is over
with the Boche well thrashed and brought to heel,
though Steelbrand serves his country still
in special duties for Intelligence.
At this very moment he approaches
the high walls which surround the castle
where von Schnitzel lurks and like a spider
weaves his web of dark malevolence.
Steelbrand scales the wall and moves towards
the tradesmen's entrance at the rear,
gliding through the darkness like a shadow.
Once inside he makes his way towards
the library where von Schnitzel waits and smiles.
The Englishman is brave enough but foolish.
He will fall into the trap.
The hunchback watches from his hiding-place
beneath the stairs. He sees the Englishman approach,
a cautious silhouette. He holds his breath,
prepares to pounce, then leaps upon his prey.
But Steelbrand is not easily dispatched.
He strikes the snarling villain with a well-timed blow
and sends him sprawling. Quickly he whips out
the strong cord from his pocket and with cool
efficiency he binds the hunchback in a trice
at wrists and ankles, leaves him trussed and gagged,

and climbs the stairs with swift athletic stride,
flings wide the library door and once again
is face to face with his old enemy.
Von Schnitzel rises calmly from his chair
and speaks in silky tones: 'Good evening Major Steelbrand,
I was expecting you. Please raise your hands.'
Steelbrand's stare into the Luger's muzzle
is unwavering. He has faced death too frequently
to be alarmed by one more Hunnish threat.
'You win,' he says, and starts to raise his hands
but in one lithe and fluid movement hurls
himself towards von Schnitzel's knees
and brings him crashing down. The German fires.
The bullet, harmless, finds the library wall.
He drops the Luger and the conflict starts.
Despite his gross physique von Schnitzel, too,
possesses massive strength. He struggles free,
regains his feet and aims a vicious kick,
below the belt, of course, which Steelbrand,
also rising, cleverly evades,
'Infernal cad!' the angry Britisher snaps,
'You'll pay for that!' and in a flash
delivers one straight left which squarely lands
upon his adversary's jaw. The German falls.
Steelbrand has the Luger now.
'We have some matters to discuss,' he says.
'Get on your feet, your hands above your head.
The game is up my friend. Your plot *kaput*.'
But he is not aware that, silently,
behind his back, the handle of the door
is slowly turning. The game is still afoot.

iv

Spy Story, or Loosely Speaking

A wet night in Old Compton Street;
the clip-joints and the porn-shops smear
the drizzling dark with yellow light,
and no one spares a second glance
for the man of middle age and size
who, limping slightly, moves towards
the newsagents and goes inside.

Felix Saddler waits upstairs
and hears the slurred iambic step
on bare and creaking boards and knows
Charles Loosely has arrived on time.
He pours two single malts and smiles
as Loosely's head peers round the door.
'It's good to see you Charles,' he says.
'Sit down, let's hear the latest score.'

Loosely takes his seat and sips
his malt and nods and then he speaks:
'You won't be too surprised to hear
that "Nimrod" is wrapped up at last.
Once Petrie's cover had been blown
I knew the handwriting and guessed
they'd snared him with a honey-trap,
and I was right. We shut up shop.
Pavement-artists kept an eye
on his old letter-box and drop.
We sent the babysitters home
when everything was clear as day.
I knew the rot was bound to come
once redbrick people were let in.
The talent-spotters must be mad –
next thing, we'll find them focusing
on sixth-form Comprehensive oiks.

We're old hands Felix, you and I,
and know how hush-hush outfits play.
There had to be a mole, of course,
and all the signs led back to base;
each signal, coded or *en clair*,
said just one thing: like chastity
betrayal starts at you-know-where.'

Felix Saddler's face is white
and suddenly his eyes are bright
with knowledge or perhaps with pain.
He says, 'You mean to say the mole ...'
and leaves the question hanging there.

Loosely nods just once; his face
shows no expression. 'Yes, the mole
is who it always had to be.'

'Not Angelino or the Pole?'
asks Felix Saddler hopelessly.

A faint smile plays on Loosely's lips:
'I think you know Control's the mole.'

'The mole? Control!'

                    'Control's the mole.
Come Felix, we have things to do.
It's time, I think, we took a stroll.'

My New Book

It's scheduled to be published in July.
The bids to serialise are running high
And movie rights were snapped up weeks ago
For what you might describe as mega-dough.
The TV channels scramble in a queue
To book me for a prime-time interview
And all the major bookstores want to fix
Signing sessions here and in the sticks.
Wait till you see the jacket! David's done
A kind of symphony of sea and sun
With subtle hints of sexuality
And darker shades of our mortality.
What's that you said? What is the book about?
You'll have to stick around to find that out,
But not for long. I'll finish it, no sweat.
I've never failed to meet a deadline yet.

Makers and Creatures

It is a curious experience
And one you're bound to know, though probably
In other realms than that of literature,
Though I speak of poems now, assuming
That you are interested, otherwise,
Of course, you wouldn't be reading this;
It is strange to come across a poem
In a magazine or book and fail
At first to see that it's your own.
Sometimes you think, grateful and surprised,
'That's really not too bad', or gloomily:
'Many have done as well and far, far better'.
Or, in despair, 'My God, that's terrible.
What was I thinking of to publish it!'
And then you start to wonder how the great
Poets felt, seeing, surprised, their poems
As strangers, beautiful. And how do all the
Makers feel to see their creatures live?
The carpenter, the architect, the man who
Crochets intricate embroideries
Of steel across the sky. And how does God
Feel, looking at his poems, his creatures?
The swelling inhalation of plump hills,
Plumage of poplars on the pale horizon,
Fishleap flashing in pools cool as silver,
Great horses haunched with glossy muscles,
Birds who spray their song like apple juice,
And the soft shock of snow. He must feel good
Surprised again by these. But what happens

When he takes a look at man? Does he say,
'That's really not too bad', or does he, as I fear,
Wince once and mutter to himself:
'What was I thinking of publishing that one?'

Likenesses

What did He really look like?
None of the gospels says.
The holy shroud of Turin
Is a kind of paraphrase

Of all those long-nosed gloomies
From Byzantium and Rome.
Blake was quite convinced
We should look much closer to home.

'Spindle-nosed rascals,' he called them,
Those images of Our Lord,
Travesties of the features
Of the Messiah he adored.

'Jesus Christ was a snubby,'
Blake asseverated, no doubt
With a sidelong glance in the looking-glass
At his own diminutive snout.

Ice Bucket

'... *all the wedding gifts were on display,*
and guess what William's Uncle Peter sent –
not something that we'd bring out every day,
but sweet of him, he's such an innocent –
an ice-bucket! Oh no, you silly thing,
not 'nice'! I said the word quite clearly, 'ice'!
Hugh managed somehow not to lose the ring.
I'm glad they threw confetti and not rice
like years ago they did ...'

                              attention strayed
as Annie's avian voice went twittering on
and I reflected on that bucket made
of glittering ice and, after she had gone,
regretted that I'd not discovered more
about this frozen artefact which could
serve as a poetic metaphor
though not, perhaps, one easily understood,
if hardly as a practical device
for drawing water and for washing floors.
It might be fun – though purchased at a price –
to set about some ordinary chores
and fill it with hot water and then see
its slow becoming its own burden till
contents and container all ran free
in one expanding flood of overspill
requiring a prosaic bucket made
of plastic or of metal to convey
the shining thing, once lovely, now betrayed,
outside the kitchen to be sluiced away.

Junk

It was a leisure-day, called 'holiday'
Only by the very few and old
Though none of these could quite remember why
The word had once possessed a gleam of gold
And still awakened distant silver sounds.
The city glittered; citizens patrolled
The areas reserved for exercise.
Among those walking in the public grounds
A young man and his son, a child of eight,
Moved towards that section of the town
Preserved by civic law in just that state
It wore in 1985, a place
For tourists, amateurs of history
And relic-hunters. There, the man and boy
Stood before a window which displayed
Disordered curiosa: garments, toys,
Primitive machines, containers made
From substances of unknown origin,
Crude metal weapons that, in ancient wars,
Were operated manually. A skin
Of extinct animal, that once was worn
For warmth, and also as a mark of caste,
By someone's female forebear, now adorned
A cabinet composed of genuine wood.
But of that dusty salvage from the past
One object seized the boy's attention: shaped
Like an oblong box, its lifted lid
Showed no interior but solid stuff
In slender layers. Its contents were itself.

The puzzled child said to his father, 'Look!
What's that thing over there?'
                              The father's brow
Showed momentary perplexity, then cleared:
'Oh that. I think it's what they called a book.'
'What did they use it for?' the child inquired.
'I'm not quite sure. I think my grandpa told me
Long ago, but I've forgotten now.'

England

A patriotic poem

Some call her Mother, but I feel
More like a husband than a son.
I need her, I suppose, but not
With ardour and she irritates
More often than she pleases me;
And only when I'm flirting with
Some hot exotic charmer do
I start to value her good points,
And then, of course, with itching guilt.
She nags. Just when you're feeling good
And one more drink would do the trick
She says: 'That's all. You know you'll make
An idiot of yourself. You might
Start dancing or reciting poems.'
Then there are moments when she kicks
Her heels and all my previous
Impressions of her character
Moonhigh. But these are rather rare.
Sometimes I've slipped away from her
And lolled with strangers in the sun,
But then I find I'm missing her.
And though she looks so stern in those
Hoarse tweeds and stomping shoes she wears
On most occasions, yet there are
Sudden times and places when
She looks so beautiful you want
To say you'd give your life for her,
Almost sure the words are true.
And yet, well, probably the next

Week or even day you'll find her
Back to normal, dressed in hessian,
Whining like a carpet-sweeper –
You'd hardly credit she can sing!
There's one thing though, she always makes
Certain that you're comfortable,
Sees your underwear is laundered,
Feeds you on a balanced diet.
But there's the snag. It's dull. And yet
You can be sure – however wild –
She'd never stick a knife in you.
We've had our rows like everyone,
Some bitter; but despite my threats
I've never seriously thought
Of getting a divorce. For one
Thing it would cost too much;
Besides, I don't think I could live
For any length of time without
My – yes, there is no other word
But I must whisper it – my love.

Dominoes

i

This is a good game:
Black clatter. Turn one over,
Small, starry midnight.

ii

The gentlest of games:
No complaints of domino
Hooliganism.

iii

Medals are not won.
No one has been known to knock
Spots off anyone.

iv

Old men in corners,
Caps, mufflers, glasses of mild;
Clicking of old bones.

Coup de Grâce

The hurt will carry you beyond all pain.
Duck if you can but, if you move too late,
The big fist zooming in can't strike again.

No matter how religiously you train
To tip the scales at your best fighting-weight
The hurt will carry you beyond all pain.

Just one brief brilliant starburst in the brain,
Then darkness drowns ambition, love and hate;
The big fist zooming in can't strike again.

You always knew one blow would end your reign
So if, tonight, this proves to be your fate,
The hurt will carry you beyond all pain.

This is the way things are: you can't complain
That insult comes with mercy on one plate;
The big fist zooming in can't strike again.

All words of consolation must seem vain,
And yet I see some cause to celebrate:
The hurt will carry you beyond all pain;
The big fist zooming in can't strike again.

Taking a Dive

'Stand up and be counted!' they said.
'Be resolute and strong!'
There was only one of me
So the counting wouldn't take long;
But, all the same, I lacked
As ever both bottle and clout,
So I lay down and was counted
                    Out.